The Sahabiyat

During the Prophet's Era

sall'Allahu ᶜalaihi wa sallam

by
Jameelah Jones

Ta-Ha Publishers Ltd.
1, Wynne Road
London SW9 0BB

Copyright © Rabee' ath-Thani 1415/October 1994, Ta-Ha Publishers Ltd.

Published by

Ta-Ha Publishers Ltd.
1 Wynne Road
London SW9 0BB
UK

All rights reserved. No part of this publication may be reproduced, stored in any retrieval system, or transmitted in any form or by any means, electronic or otherwise, without written permission of the publishers.

By: Jameelah Jones
General Editor: Afsar Siddiqui
Edited by: Abdassamad Clarke

British Library Cataloguing in Publication Data
Jones, Jameelah
Sahabiyat, During The Prophet's Era, The
I. Title

ISBN: 1 897940 23 8

Typeset by: BookWright, Isle of Lewis. Tel: 0851-870198.
Printed by: Deluxe Printers, London. Tel: 081-965 1771

For 10–15 years old

Contents

Foreword 5
Nusaybah Umm ʿImarah 6
Sumayyah bint Khayyat 11
Umm Salamah 13
Safiyyah bint ʿAbdu'l-Muttalib 19
Ruqayyah bint Muhammad 22
ʿAtikah bint Nafil 24
Asma' bint Abu Bakr 27
Zaynab bint Muhammad 30
Umm Sulaim bint Milhan 35

Foreword

It might be wise to view the lives of some of the *Sahabiyat* (female companions) of the Prophet Muhammad, *salla'llahu ᶜalaihi wa sallam*, during the era in which Islam was nascent, to determine the breadth and depth of women's roles. In my view, the few examples which follow are a testimony to the vibrancy of Islam and the essential spiritual equality which exists between men and women in Islam. One sees that Muslim women were able to rise to the occasion when the situation demanded it. These women were the counterparts of their men – courageous, strong, thoughtful and ready to give all for the cause of truth.

Women usually carried water, nursed the wounded, and buried the dead during times of war; however, it was not absolutely unheard of for women to go forth into battle as was the case of Umm ᶜImarah, Kanza and a few others.

Muslim women also encouraged their husbands to stand up for truth against the unbelievers and invited non-Muslim men who loved them to consider the message of Islam and enter the fold. Thus, we would like to present a few stories of the early women of Islam.

Jameelah Jones
1990

Nusaybah Umm ᶜImarah
bint Kaᶜb ibn Auf Al-Ansariyah, radiyAllahu ᶜanha

Umm ᶜImarah was an important Companion and a great fighter for Allah's cause. She was right-acting, ardent and devoted. She exerted herself for Allah, relying only on Him.

Nusaybah bint Kaᶜb converted to Islam during the early days. She was present at the second Pledge of *Al-ᶜAqabah* at which she swore allegiance to the Prophet, may Allah bless him and grant him peace, along with her first husband, Zaid ibn ᶜAsim who died after the Battle of *Badr*.

She was also present at the Battle of *Uhud* with her second husband, Ghaziyah ibn ᶜAmr and her sons, ᶜAbdullah and Habib. They left early in the morning so that she could give water to the injured. Nusaybah had brought a sword, a bow and a quiver of arrows, in addition to her water skin and bandages. Not long after the battle had begun, she reached the place where the Prophet, may Allah bless him and grant him peace, had taken up his position on relatively high ground. He was with some of his closest companions and the battle was going in favour of the Muslims.

The Muslims continued to advance until the way into the enemy camp was open. They were tempted by the booty and began to surge into the enemy camp seeking plunder. The fifty archers chosen to guard the rear of the

Nusaybah Umm ʿImarah

army saw their companions taking spoils of war and felt that they would lose out. So, totally neglecting the Prophet's command not to leave their posts no matter what happened, they left, assuming that the battle was finished. Their commander, ʿAbdullah ibn Jubair, was left with only a few archers.

When the enemy realised what was happening, they set off for the post where the archers were stationed and killed the remaining few. Then the enemy cavalry attacked the unguarded ranks of the believers. Some of Quraysh, who had begun to flee, rejoined the battle. Some Muslims lost heart and began to run away. Many faithful Muslims fought on, but the tide had turned against them, and they were pushed back step by step.

Once Nusaybah realised that the Muslims were being defeated she joined the Prophet with a sword, a bow and her quiver full of arrows. She began shooting arrows until they were all used up. Ibn Qamiʿah, a man from one of the clans from the outskirts of Makkah, was shouting, "Where is Muhammad? May I not survive if he survives." Then Ibn Qamiʿah recognised the Prophet and struck at him. The blow was averted by Talhah, who was standing next to the Prophet. Talhah then threw himself in the direction of the sword and the Muslims closed in around the Prophet to protect him. Umm ʿImarah was a part of the human barrier which protected the Prophet. Ibn Qamiʿah struck her and she struck him, but he was wearing two coats of armour which protected him from her blows.

Umm ʿImarah had the following to say about the Battle of *Uhud*, "The people had left the Prophet exposed and only a few, not more than ten, remained and my husband, my sons and I myself were among them. We defended him and the people were moving around in a defeated state. I did not have my shield with me. The Prophet, may Allah bless him and grant him peace, saw a man with a shield, so he said, 'Give your shield to someone who is fighting.' So the man gave his shield to me and I used it to defend the Prophet."

So Nusaybah continued fighting, treating the wounded and carrying water for them. Her son was wounded and his blood began to flow. However, she was totally oblivious to her son's condition until the Prophet, may Allah bless him and grant him peace, said, "Bandage your wounded." Thereupon, she went to her son and wrapped the wound while the Prophet, may Allah bless him and grant him peace, stood looking at her. After she had bandaged the wound, she said to her son, "Rise and fight the people."

The Prophet said, may Allah bless him and grant him peace, "And who is capable of bearing what you bear, Umm ʿImarah?"

The Prophet, may Allah bless him and grant him peace, used to say, "The position of Nusaybah today is better than so and so. I saw her on the Day of *Uhud* fighting fiercely and she had wrapped her dress around her waist as an obstruction. She had been wounded thirteen times." He used to say, "I saw Ibn Qamiʿah striking her on her shoulders, and her most serious would took one year to heal."

The people thought well of Nusaybah also. When ʿUmar ibn Al-Khattab came with some very fine cloth, some people said, "Surely, this cloth is worth such and such. Why don't you send it to Safiyah bint ʿUbaidah, the wife of ʿAbdullah ibn ʿUmar?" Someone else said, "Send it to one who has more right to it than her, Umm

ʿImarah, Nusaybah bint Kaʿb, for I heard the Prophet say, may Allah bless him and grant him peace, 'On the Day of *Uhud*, whether I looked to the right or the left, I saw Nusaybah fighting round about me.'"

She was present at the Pledge of *Ridwan*, when the Muslims swore to stand by the Prophet to the death. That was because they were concerned about ʿUthman's prolonged absence when he went to negotiate with Quraysh while the Prophet, may Allah bless him and grant him peace, and other Companions waited at *Hudaybiyah*. Indeed, rumours circulated that ʿUthman, may Allah be pleased with him, had treacherously been killed by the Makkans.

Nusaybah then later took part in the fighting against Musailimah in *Yamamah*. She went to Abu Bakr who was *Khalifah* at the time, to seek permission to join the expedition with Khalid against Musailimah. Abu Bakr said, may Allah be pleased with him, "We know your worth in war, so go out, in the name of Allah." Abu Bakr committed her to Khalid ibn Al-Walid's charge and she fought bravely at *Yamamah*. She was wounded in eleven different places and had her hand chopped off. Her son, Habib, was killed.

After Musailimah had been defeated and killed and the war was over, Nusaybah returned to her house. Khalid ibn al-Walid came there to treat her hand with hot oil, to seal the wound and stop the bleeding. The hot oil was even more painful than having the hand cut off.

There is a story that ʿIkrimah narrated, that Nusaybah went to the Prophet, may Allah bless him and grant him peace, and said, "I see that everything goes to men, and I do not see anything mentioned for women." Then the verse was revealed:

Sahabiyat

"For Muslim men and Muslim women, for believing men and believing women, for devout men and devout women, for truthful men and truthful women, for patient men and patient women, for men and women who humble themselves, for men and women who give *sadaqah*, for fasting men and fasting women, for men who guard their private parts and women who guard, and for men who remember Allah much and women who remember, Allah has prepared for them forgiveness and a great reward."
(Surah Ahzab 33: 35)

Sumayyah bint Khayyat

radiy'Allahu ʿanha

Sumayyah was a great woman who possessed strong faith in Allah. She accepted Islam in Makkah, and was the seventh of the first seven to enter Islam.

Yasir was a confederate of Abu Hudhaifah of the Bani Makhzum. He married Sumayyah, who was one of the slaves of Abu Hudhaifah.

Sumayyah, Yasir and ʿAmmar, their son, were poor. They had no tribe or family to support them or come to their aid. ʿAmmar heard the Prophet's message, listened to the Qur'an and he and his parents believed in the revelation sent to the Prophet, may Allah bless him and grant him peace. To take such a stand in the early days of Islam when few believed or were willing to follow the Prophet shows that they had very strong *Iman*.

She was persecuted terribly by the polytheists of Makkah although she was an old woman at the time. Despite torture visited on her by Quraysh she did not renounce Islam. Quraysh used to torture ʿAmmar, Yasir, and Sumayyah herself on an open plain called *Ramda'*.

The Prophet, may Allah bless him and grant him peace, passed them one day and told them to be patient as they were promised Paradise. ʿAmmar said, "O Prophet, we've experienced the extremity of torture." The Prophet, may Allah bless him and grant him peace, said,

"Patience, O Abu'l-Yaqdhan; Allah will not punish any member of the family of Yasir by fire."

Then one day Abu Jahl pierced Sumayyah through the heart and she died. All of this took place before the migration to Madinah. Quraysh tortured Sumayyah and Yasir until they martyred them, but the two of them refused to give up their faith in Allah.

When Abu Jahl was killed during the Battle of *Badr*, the Prophet, may Allah bless him and grant him peace, said to ʿAmmar, "Allah has killed your mother's murderer."

Sumayyah was the first to be killed for the sake of Allah in Islam; however not all Muslims were able to withstand the torture which Quraysh inflicted. Some found themselves saying anything at all to gain their release from torture. Allah acknowledges with mercy, those who say things against Islam even going back on their *shahadah* though belief is still in their hearts, in this *ayah*:

"Anyone who, after accepting faith in Allah, utters unbelief, except under compulsion his heart remaining firm in belief; but such as open their breast to unbelief, on them is wrath from Allah, and theirs will be a dreadful punishment."
(*Surah An-Nahl* 16: 106)

Umm Salamah

Hind bint Abi Umayyah ibn Al-Mughirah radiy'Allahu ᶜanha

Hind was an eminent *Muhajirah*, who possessed intelligence, integrity, maturity and beauty. She emigrated to Abyssinia and Madinah for the sake of Allah. Her camel-borne sedan was the first to enter Madinah from Makkah.

She was married to Abu Salamah ᶜAbdullah ibn ᶜAbdu'l-Asad, who was Abu Talib's nephew. Abu Salamah sought Abu Talib's protection from Quraysh when he accepted Islam. When this happened, Abu Salamah's tribe, the Bani Makhzum, went to Abu Talib and said, "You are protecting your nephew, Muhammad, from us but why are you protecting our tribesman?" Abu Talib replied, "He asked for my protection, and he is my sister's son." At this Abu Lahab stood up and said, "O Quraysh, you have continually attacked this Shaykh for giving his protection among his own people. By Allah, you must stop this or we will stand with him until he gains his object." The people stopped protesting because they did not want to annoy Abu Lahab who was their chief supporter against the Prophet.

Abu Salamah, may Allah be pleased with him, went to Madinah a year before the Pledge at *Al-ᶜAqabah*, after having emigrated to Abyssinia previously. He migrated to Madinah because Quraysh were treating him badly and also because he had heard that some of the people of Madinah had accepted Islam.

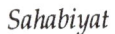

Umm Salamah, may Allah be pleased with her, said that when Abu Salamah decided to set out for Madinah, he saddled his camel for her, mounted her on it with her son, Salamah, then set out leading the camel. When the men of Bani Al-Mughirah of Bani Makhzum saw him, they got up and said, "So far as you are concerned, you can do what you like, but what about your wife? Do you suppose that we shall let you take her away?" So they snatched the camel's reins from his hand and took Hind from him. Abu Salamah's family, the Bani ʿAbdu'l-Asad, were angry at this and said, "We will not leave our son with her seeing you have torn her from our tribesman." So they dragged her little boy, Salamah, so forcefully that they dislocated his arm, and took him away, while the Bani Al-Mughirah kept Umm Salamah with them, and Abu Salamah went to Madinah.

Thus, Umm Salamah, may Allah be pleased with her, was separated from both her husband and her son. She used to go out every morning and sit in the valley weeping continuously. When a year had passed, one of her cousins belonging to the Bani Al-Mughirah passed, saw her plight and took pity on her. He said to his tribesmen, "Why don't you let this woman go? You have separated husband, wife and child." So they said to her, "You may rejoin your husband if you like." She saddled her camel, took her son in her arms and set out making for Madinah, not a soul with her. She thought that she could get food from anyone whom she met on the road until she reached her husband.

When she was in *Tanʿim* (about six miles from Makkah), she met ʿUthman ibn Talha ibn Abi Talha, brother of Bani

ʿAbdu'd-Dar, who asked her where she was going and if she were all alone. She told him that except for Allah and her little boy she was entirely alone. He said that she ought not to be left alone and helpless like that. Then he took hold of her camel's halter and went along with her.

Umm Salamah later said, "Never have I met an Arab more noble than him." When they halted, he would make the camel kneel for her and then go away from her. When they reached a stopping place, he would lead her camel away, unload it, and tie it to a tree. Then he would go a distance from her and lie under a tree. When evening came, he would bring the camel, tell her to mount, and when she was firmly established in the saddle, he would take the halter and lead it until he brought her to a halt. He did this all the way to Madinah. When he saw the village of Bani ʿAmr ibn ʿAuf in *Quba*, he said, "Your husband is in this village, so enter it with the blessing of Allah." Then he went off on his way back to Makkah. Umm Salamah used to say, "By Allah, I do not know a family in Islam which suffered what the family of Salamah did, nor have I seen a nobler man than ʿUthman ibn Talha."

Once Umm Salamah said to Abu Salamah, may Allah be pleased with them, "I have been told that if a woman's husband dies and he is one of the inhabitants of Paradise and she does not marry after him, Allah will join them in Paradise. And likewise, if a woman dies first and the husband is left." Umm Salamah said, "I'll not marry after you." Abu Salamah said, "Marry after me if I die first." He prayed, "O Allah, grant Umm Salamah a better man than me and do not let her be harmed."

Sahabiyat

In another version, the narrator said that when Umm Salamah was nursing Abu Salamah after the Battle of *Badr*, he said to her: I heard the Messenger of Allah, may Allah bless him and grant him peace, say, "Whenever a calamity afflicts anyone, he should say: 'Truly, we belong to Allah and to to Him we are returning.' And he would pray, 'O Lord, grant me something good from it which only You, Exalted and Mighty, can give.'"

Abu Salamah fought in the Battle of *Badr*, in which the Muslims were victorious and in the Battle of *Uhud*, in which he was severely wounded, eventually dying from those wounds. The Prophet, may Allah bless him and grant him peace, visited Abu Salamah during his final illness and was with him when he died. He prayed for Abu Salamah, "O Lord, forgive Abu Salamah. Raise him up among those who are near You. Let someone among those who survive him fill his place. Forgive us and him, O Lord of the Worlds. Widen his grave and enlighten it for him."

When Umm Salamah had completed the waiting period for widows of four months and ten days, Abu Bakr proposed to her. She refused his proposal. Then ʿUmar proposed and she turned him down too. When the Prophet, may Allah bless him and grant him peace, proposed to her, she said, "O Messenger of Allah, I have three characteristics. I am a woman who is extremely jealous, and I am afraid that you will see in me something that will anger you and cause Allah to punish me. I am a woman who is already advanced in age, and I am a woman who has young children." The Prophet, may Allah bless him and grant him peace, replied, "As for the jealousy, I pray Allah to let it go away from you. As for the question of

Umm Salamah

age, I am afflicted with the same problem as you. As for your children, your family is my family."

So she married the Prophet who gave her a bed stuffed with palm-leaves, a bowl, a dish and a handmill. When the Prophet, may Allah bless him and grant him peace, came to spend the wedding night with her, he said, "Do not feel that you are unimportant among your people, for if you wish, I will spend seven days (with you) and seven days with the rest of my wives, or if you wish, I will spend three days with you and divide the time equally after that." She said, "Make it three."

The Prophet, may Allah bless him and grant him peace, married Umm Salamah during the sixth year of the *Hijrah*. ᶜA'ishah, may Allah be pleased with her, was quite upset when she heard people talking about how beautiful Umm Salamah was. However, when ᶜA'ishah saw her, she said, "By Allah, she is not as beautiful as they said."

The Messenger of Allah, may Allah bless him and grant him peace, used to visit his wives, one by one, after he prayed ᶜ*Asr*. He always started with Umm Salamah, because she was the eldest, and ended with ᶜA'ishah, the youngest.

Umm Salamah was a wise woman and a good advisor. She counselled the Prophet on the Day of *Hudaybiyah*, when he made a treaty with the people of Makkah. The Muslims had set out to perform an ᶜ*Umrah*, bringing animals to sacrifice in Makkah. After the agreement had been made and he, may Allah bless him and grant him peace, had agreed not to perform the ᶜ*Umrah* that year, he told the Companions to sacrifice their animals and cut or shave their hair. But not one man got up, even

Sahabiyat

after he had told them to do so three times. They had been very shocked at how generous the Prophet had been to the Makkans in making the agreement. The Messenger of Allah, may Allah bless him and grant him peace, went to Umm Salamah and told her what had happened. She said to him, "If you want them to do that, you must leave them and not say a word to any of them until you have slaughtered your animals and called your barber to shave your head."

The Prophet, may Allah bless him and grant him peace, followed her suggestion. He left the group of Companions without speaking to anyone, slaughtered his animals and called his barber to shave his hair. When the Companions, may Allah be pleased with them, saw this, they all arose and slaughtered their animals and began shaving each other so eagerly that they were in danger of killing each other, out of anxiety.

Umm Salamah took part in the Conquest of *Khaibar* and said, "I wish that Allah had made *jihad* obligatory for us as he did for men, and that we would receive the same reward." Then the following *ayah* was revealed:

"Do not seek that with which Allah has favoured some of you over others."

Umm Salamah narrated *hadith* directly from the Prophet, may Allah bless him and grant him peace, and from Abu Salamah, and Fatimah Az-Zahra', may Allah be pleased with them all. She died in the year 59 AH or 61 AH when she was eighty-four years old. Abu Hurayrah prayed the funeral prayer over her and she was buried in *Al-Baqi^c*.

Safiyyah bint ʿAbduʾl-Muttalib

radiyʾAllahu ʿanha

Safiyyah, may Allah be pleased with her, was the aunt of the Prophet, may Allah bless him and grant him peace. She and Hamza were children of Hala, wife of ʿAbduʾl-Muttalib. Hala had been ʿAbduʾl-Muttalib's last wife and the wedding had taken place on the same day as the wedding of the Prophet's parents.

Safiyyah was a great lady, who accepted Islam early and took the oath of allegiance to the Prophet, may Allah bless him and grant him peace, and then migrated to Madinah. Before Islam, she had been married to Harith ibn Harb ibn ʿUmayyah. Then she married Al-ʿAwwam ibn Khuwaylid ibn Asad, who was the brother of Khadijah, the Prophet's wife. She had Az-Zubayr, As-Saib and ʿAbduʾl-Kaʿbah by Al-ʿAwwam.

She was present at the Battle of *Uhud* when the Muslims suffered defeat. At one stage in the battle, she stood up with a lance in her hand and said, "Are you trying to defeat the Prophet, may Allah bless him and grant him peace?" She waved the lance in the enemies' faces. When the Prophet, may Allah bless him and grant him peace, saw her, he told her son Az-Zubayr to take her back because he did not want her to see her brother, Hamza, who had been killed during the battle. Az-Zubayr met her and told her that the Prophet, may Allah bless him and grant him peace, had ordered her to go back. She asked, "Why? I have heard that my brother has been mutilated and that has happened for Allah's sake. He, the Most High, has fully reconciled us to what has happened. I will remain calm and patient if Allah wills." When Az-Zubayr returned to the Prophet and reported this to him, he, may Allah bless him and grant him peace, told him to leave her alone. So she came and looked on Hamza and prayed over him and said, "Truly, we belong to Allah and we are returning to Him." She asked Allah's forgiveness for him. Then the Prophet, may Allah bless him and grant him peace, ordered the Muslims to bury Hamza.

She took part in the Battle of the *Khandaq* (the Trench). When the Prophet, may Allah bless him and grant him peace, went to the battle, he put his wives and womenfolk in a fortress which belonged to Hassan ibn Thabit. A Jewish man walked around the fortress when the women were inside. The Jews had broken their treaty with the Prophet and were acting with the enemies of Islam. So, Safiyyah said, "O Hassan, this Jew is going around the fortress and the Prophet, may Allah bless him and grant him peace, and his companions are busy, so go down and kill him." Hassan said, "May Allah forgive you, you know that I cannot be involved in this." So when Safiyyah heard what Hassan had to say, she got up and took a pole. She went down and out of the fortress to the Jew, hit him with the pole and killed him. On her return to the fortress, she said to Hassan, "Go down and strip him of his weapons and clothes. I would strip him, but he is a man." Hassan said, "I have no need to strip him, O daughter of ʿAbdu'l-Muttalib." She also participated in the Battle of *Khaybar*.

Safiyyah bint ʿAbdu'l-Muttalib

ʿUmar ibn Al-Khattab allocated 6,000 *dirhams*, as a yearly stipend, for her during his *khilafah*. She narrated *hadith* from the Prophet, may Allah bless him and grant him peace, and others narrated from her. She was a great poetess and recited poetry on the deaths of her father and her brother, Hamza.

Safiyyah died during the *khilafah* of ʿUmar in the year 26 AH when she was 73 years old. ʿUmar buried her in *Al-Baqiʿ*, the cemetery of Madinah. However some others say that she died in the *khilafah* of ʿUthman.

The original Bab Makkah, the Makkah gate – from a photograph of the 1920s.

Ruqayyah bint Muhammad

radiy'Allahu 'anha

Ruqayyah was born almost twenty years before the *Hijrah*. She was married to ʿUtbah ibn Abu Lahab before her father first received revelation. Abu Lahab, the enemy of Allah, told his son to divorce her.

Ruqayyah, may Allah be pleased with her, accepted Islam with her mother, Khadijah, and took the oath of allegiance to the Prophet, may Allah bless him and grant him peace. Then she married ʿUthman ibn ʿAffan in Makkah and emigrated to Abyssinia and then to Madinah with him. She had become sick with measles during the period of the Battle of *Badr* and the Prophet, may Allah bless him and grant him peace, went to *Badr* and left ʿUthman behind to tend Ruqayyah. She died while the Prophet, may Allah bless him and grant him peace, was at *Badr*, during the month of Ramadan, only seventeen months after the emigration of the Prophet to Madinah.

When she died the women cried over her. ʿUmar came along and started beating them. The Prophet, may Allah bless him and grant him peace, grabbed his hand and said, "Let them cry, ʿUmar. They cry and the devil screeches, for what comes from the eyes and the heart is from Allah and His mercy. That which comes from the hands and the tongue is from *Shaytan.*" (Meaning that women should not beat their chests and wail in mourning).

Her sister, Fatimah, may Allah be pleased with her, sat on the edge of the grave next to the Prophet and started to cry. The Prophet, may Allah bless him and grant him peace, wiped her tears away with the edge of his robe. Anas ibn Malik, may Allah be pleased with him, narrated, "We witnessed the burial of the daughter of Muhammad, and the Prophet, may Allah bless him and grant him peace, sat by the grave and we saw tears fill his eyes."

▲ Mosque of the Prophet, Medina

ʿAtikah bint Nafil

radiy'Allahu ʿanha

During the early years of Islam, women encouraged their husbands to go forward for the cause of Islam. These women, like their men, were courageous, strong and thoroughly ready to give all for the sake of truth. The *Sahabiyat* had personalities which cannot be scoffed at. Here is a story of one such of the early women of Islam.

ʿAtikah bint ʿAmr ibn Nafil was one of the most beautiful women of Quraysh. She married ʿAbdurrahman ibn Abi Bakr, who was extremely fearful of Allah, handsome and considerate of his parents. ʿAbdurrahman was very much in love with ʿAtikah. One day his father passed by and visited him in his home. When he saw how taken his son was with ʿAtikah, he advised him to divorce her, as she had run away with his reason and overcome his senses. ʿAbdurrahman told his father that he was not able to do it. His father said, "I adjure you to do so." Since ʿAbdurrahman was not humanly able to oppose his father he divorced his wife. However, after the divorce, he became extremely unhappy and even stopped eating and drinking. When Abu Bakr went to him one day, but his son did not even notice him, he realised that his son was totally devastated by the divorce. ʿAbdurrahman was lying in the sun reciting the following verses:

ᶜAtikah bint Nafil

> I swear by Allah that I will never forget you
>> As long as the sun rises
>> And as long as the ring-necked dove coos.
>
> I cannot imagine one such as me divorcing one like her
>> Nor one like her being divorced without any reason
> She is chaste, religious and noble
>> She has a balanced personality and a logical mind.

After hearing this, Abu Bakr advised his son to take her back. ᶜAbdurrahman obeyed his father and they were reunited. ᶜAtikah remained with him until he was killed by an arrow while out with the Prophet, may Allah bless him and grant him peace, on the Day of Ta'if.

ᶜAtikah later married ᶜUmar during his *khilafah*. Their union ended with his death at the hands of an assassin. Some time passed, then Az-Zubayr ibn Al-ᶜAwwam proposed to her and subsequently married her.

It was ᶜAtikah's custom to leave the house so that she could pray in the mosque. Az-Zubayr was possessive. It upset him to see her leaving the house to pray in the mosque. He appealed to her to stop, but she saw no reason to give up praying in the mosque in which she had prayed behind the Prophet, may Allah bless him and grant him peace, Abu Bakr and ᶜUmar.

Az-Zubayr knew that he should not forbid her from praying in the Prophet's mosque, because he knew the *hadith* in which the Prophet, may Allah bless him and grant him peace, had said, "Do not forbid Allah's female slaves (attending) His mosque." So one night when she went out to the mosque, Az-Zubayr hid himself in a place where she could not see him and, as she passed by, he

Sahabiyat

hit at her. After that incident, she decided not to go out to the mosque anymore. He would say to her, "Aren't you going out, ᶜAtikah?" She would reply, "I used to go out (to pray) when people were people and they didn't want to harm anyone, but now, I'll not go."

Then Az-Zubayr was martyred and she subsequently married Muhammad ibn Abu Bakr, who was killed in Egypt. At this point, she declared that she would never marry anyone else after him, for fear that he too would be martyred. She once said, "If I were to marry all the inhabitants of the earth, they would all be killed." She was given the affectionate name, *Zawjah Ash-Shuhada'*, the wife of the martyrs.

the Muslim quarter, Jerusalem

Asma' bint Abu Bakr

radiy'Allahu ʿanhuma

The story of Asma' bint Abi Bakr is a story of bravery, faith and human endeavour. She was one of the great female companions of the Prophet, may Allah bless him and grant him peace. Asma' was born twenty-seven years before the *Hijrah*. Her father, Abu Bakr As Siddiq, may Allah be pleased with him, was one of a kind. He was one of the vanguard of Islam, first *Khalifah* of the Muslims and one of the best of creation after the prophets. He was the closest companion of the Prophet. Qutailah bint ʿAbdul-ʿUzza, a Qurayshi lady from the tribe of Bani ʿAmir ibn Luwiyah, was Asma's mother.

Abu Bakr, may Allah be pleased with him, was the first adult man to accept Islam. Needless to say, Asma' was raised in a Muslim environment. As Abu Bakr's eldest daughter, she grew to be knowledgeable, patient and steadfast in the path of Allah. She met pure, upright Muslims, intent upon upholding true values and high morals, all around her in her father's house. Certainly, it is hardly surprising that Asma' became one of the foremost figures in Islam. She accepted Islam in Makkah without hesitation. According to historians, only seventeen people preceded her in embracing Islam.

Asma' was ten years older than her sister, ʿA'ishah.

Asma' was known to be witty, intelligent, diplomatic, noble and a distinctive personality. Nothing much is known about her physical appearance other than that she was tall and attractive. She married Az-Zubayr ibn Al-ᶜAwwam, may Allah be pleased with him, one of the ten Companions promised the Garden.

Asma' was known as 'She of The Two Belts' due to the part she played in the emigration of the Prophet to Madinah. When the Prophet, may Allah bless him and grant him peace, and Abu Bakr, may Allah be pleased with him, hid in a cave in Mount *Thaur* while the *kuffar* were looking for them, Asma' brought food to them. Not having a strap to tie up the bundle with, she tore her belt, or girdle, in two and used a half to carry the food.

At that time, Abu Bakr took his entire wealth with him which was approximately 5,000 or 6,000 *dirhams*. After Abu Bakr's flight, his father came to inquire after the family and their financial situation. He was anxious for them. He was blind. Asma' took some stones, covered them with cloth and placed his hands on the bundle saying, "Feel how much he has left to take care of us." But, Abu Bakr, may Allah be pleased with him, had not left anything with them. She only wanted to reassure her grandfather about their situation.

Az-Zubayr was somewhat stern and severe with Asma', yet she bore it patiently. Once she complained to her father, and he advised her to continue to be patient, saying, "O my daughter, be patient, for if a woman is married to a good man who dies and she does not marry anyone after him, they will be joined in Paradise."

Asma' was pregnant when they emigrated to Madinah. Her son, ᶜAbdullah ibn Az-Zubayr, was the first child born to the Muslims after their emigration to Madinah. The Companions, may Allah be pleased with them, rejoiced because the Jews of Madinah claimed to have bewitched the Muslims so that they could not have any children. Allah showed the falsity of their claims with the birth of ᶜAbdullah.

Asma' lived a long full life of almost a hundred years. She narrated fifty-eight *hadith* from the Prophet, may Allah bless him and grant him peace. She lived to see her son assume the *khilafah* during a particularly turbulent period in the history of the Muslims. She lived to see her son ᶜAbdullah, may Allah be pleased with him, seek and die a hero's death at the hands of Hajjaj ibn Yusuf.

Zaynab bint Muhammad
radiy'Allahu ᶜanha

Zaynab was the second child born to the Prophet, may Allah bless him and grant him peace, and Khadijah, may Allah be pleased with her. She came to marry Abu'l-ᶜAs ibn Ar-Rabiᶜ who was the son of Hala bint Khuwaylid, Khadijah's sister. Before the revelation, Khadijah had asked the Prophet to find a wife for Abu'l-ᶜAs, who was one of the well-respected, wealthy traders of Makkah. So, the Prophet, may Allah bless him and grant him peace, married him to his daughter, Zaynab.

When prophethood descended upon Muhammad, may Allah bless him and grant him peace, Khadijah and her daughters believed in him and in his message; however Abu'l-ᶜAs did not convert. The Quraysh went to him and told him to divorce Zaynab, promising him any other woman he desired. He refused, saying that he did not want any other woman of Quraysh. The Prophet, may Allah bless him and grant him peace, always used to speak warmly of him due to the stand he took against the Quraysh.

Nevertheless, Islam had made a split between Zaynab and her husband; but little *shariᶜah* had as yet been revealed, so Abu'l-ᶜAs and Zaynab continued together as Muslim and *kafir*, wife and husband until after the *Hijrah*.

Zaynab bint Muhammad

Abu'l-ᶜAs joined the expedition to *Badr* on the side of Quraysh and was captured by the Muslims, so he remained in Madinah. ᶜA'ishah, may Allah be pleased with her, said, "When the Makkans sent the ransom for their prisoners, Zaynab (who was still in Makkah) sent the money for Abu'l-ᶜAs and, along with it, a necklace which her mother, Khadijah, had given her on her wedding. When the Prophet, may Allah bless him and grant him peace, saw this, his feelings overcame him and he said, 'If you would like her to have her captive husband back and return her money to her, do so.' The people at once agreed and they let him go and sent the money back."

However, the Prophet, may Allah bless him and grant him peace, imposed a condition on Abu'l-ᶜAs, that upon his return he should send Zaynab to Madinah. Abu'l-ᶜAs promised to honour his condition. Allah had made it clear that a Muslim woman could not be the wife of a non-Muslim man.

After Abu'l-ᶜAs returned to Makkah, he informed Zaynab of his promise to her father and they agreed that their little daughter, Umamah, should go with her. At the time, Zaynab was expecting another child. When all the preparations had been made for the journey, Abu'l-ᶜAs's brother, Kinanah was sent as an escort. Their plans had been kept secret, but they set off in broad daylight, which upset Quraysh and they decided to bring Zaynab back to Makkah. Habar ibn Al-Aswad ibn ᶜAbdu'l-Muttalib struck at her with his spear as she sat in the camel sedan. Kinanah dismounted to protect her. Then Abu Sufyan and some others asked Kinanah to discuss the matter calmly with them. Abu Sufyan argued that it was a mistake to bring Zaynab out of Makkah publicly. He said that people would take it as a sign of weakness if they allowed Zaynab to leave in broad daylight. He said that they didn't want to keep her from her father, nor did they want revenge. They asked Kinanah to take her back into Makkah and, when people stopped talking about the matter, she could steal out secretly to join her father. Kinanah accepted this proposal and they all returned to Makkah. Shortly afterwards, Zaynab miscarried due to the fright caused her by Habar.

When enough time had elapsed and she had recovered sufficiently, Kinanah took her and little Umamah under the cover of night and escorted them as far as a valley on the outskirts of Makkah. They were met by Zaid ibn Harithah who escorted them to Madinah and to the Prophet, may Allah bless him and grant him peace.

Almost five months after the Battle of Trench, a rich caravan of Quraysh was returning on its way from Syria, and Zaid was sent to waylay it with a hundred and seventy men. Zaid and his men captured the entire caravan and most of the men were taken captive. Abu'l-ᶜAs was among them; however, he managed to escape. Nevertheless, as he passed Madinah, he was filled with the desire to see his former wife and little daughter. So he entered the city under the cover of night and somehow or other found the house of his former wife. It was near the time of *Fajr* and when Bilal made the call to prayer, Zaynab went into the mosque, leaving Abu'l-ᶜAs with Umamah. After the Prophet, may Allah bless him and grant him peace, said, *"Allahu Akbar"*, and the men repeated it after him, there was a moment of silence and in this brief moment, Zaynab cried out, "O people, I give protection to Abu'l-ᶜAs." Then she too said, *"Allahu Akbar"*, and entered into the prayer.

When the Prophet, may Allah bless him and grant him

peace, had pronounced the final *"As-salamu ᶜalaikum"*, he rose and turned to face the Muslims saying, "Did you hear what I heard?" There was a general assent. He, may Allah bless him and grant him peace, said, "By Him in whose hand is my soul, I knew nothing of this until I heard what I heard. The least Muslim can grant protection which shall be binding on all other Muslims." Then he went to his daughter and said, "Receive him with honour, but let him not come to you as a husband, for you are not his, by law."

She told her father that Abu'l-ᶜAs was worried about the loss of the merchandise which he himself had acquired by barter on behalf of Quraysh who had entrusted their goods to him, for he was considered one of the most trustworthy men in Makkah. So the Prophet, may Allah bless him and grant him peace, sent word to those who had taken part in the expedition and had taken the property of Abu'l-ᶜAs that, "This man is related to us as you know, and you have taken this property of his. If you should be so good as to return it to him, that would please me, but if you will not, it is booty which Allah has given you, so that you have the better right to it."

They said that they would give it back to him and everything was returned, without exception. They noticed that there were signs that he had thoughts of entering Islam, so one of the men said to him, "Why don't you embrace Islam and take these goods for yourself, for they are not the property of idolators?" However, Abu'l-ᶜAs answered, "It would be a bad beginning to my Islam, if I betrayed my trust."

He took the goods to Makkah and gave them to their owners. Then he returned to Madinah and entered Islam, pledging his allegiance to the Prophet, may Allah bless

Sahabiyat

him and grant him peace. So Zaynab was reunited with her husband and there was great rejoicing in the family of the Prophet and throughout the city. This occurred during the seventh year of the *Hijrah*.

Zaynab died the next year, in the eighth year of the *Hijrah*. The Prophet, may Allah bless him and grant him peace, was with her at the end and spoke words of comfort to her. When the body had been prepared for burial, the Prophet, may Allah bless him and grant him peace, led the funeral prayer and prayed by her grave. He grieved deeply for her.

Umm Sulaim bint Milhan
radiyAllahu ʿanha

She was a great fighter for Allah's cause. An intelligent perceptive woman, she embraced Islam with the first Madinans to do so and took the oath of allegiance to the Prophet. Her husband, Malik ibn An-Nadir (the father of Anas ibn Malik) became very angry about her conversion and said to her, "You have become a Magian!" She said, "I am not a Magian but I believe in this man (meaning the Prophet, may Allah bless him and grant him peace)."

After Malik was killed in Syria, Abu Talha proposed to her, although he was still not a Muslim. She refused and said to him, "O Abu Talha, don't you know that the lord that you are worshipping is only stone and cannot harm or help you? Or it is merely wood brought to you by a carpenter who has carved it for you. It cannot harm you or help you. Aren't you ashamed of worshipping this?" She went on to say, "If you accept Islam, I do not want a dower from you other than your acceptance of Islam."

Shortly afterwards, Islam descended into the heart of Abu Talha and he said the *Shahadah* (he bore witness that there is no god but Allah and that Muhammad is the slave and messenger of Allah).

Abu Talha became one of the foremost fighters in the cause of Allah. Anas (Umm Sulaim's son from her first marriage), may Allah be pleased with him, reported, "On the day of the Battle of *Uhud*, the people ran away leaving the Prophet, may Allah bless him and grant him peace, but Abu Talha was defending the Prophet with his shield held in front of him. Abu Talha was a strong experienced archer who used to keep his bow strung and well stretched. On that day he broke two or three bows. If any man passed by carrying a quiver full of arrows, the Prophet, may Allah bless him and grant him peace, would say to him, 'Empty it in front of Abu Talha.' When the Prophet started looking at the enemy by raising his head, Abu Talha said, 'O Messenger of Allah! Let my parents be sacrificed for your sake! Please don't raise your head and make it visible, in case an arrow of the enemy hits you. Let my neck and chest be wounded instead of yours.'"

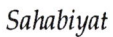

Umm Sulaim was also present at the Battle of *Uhud*. She brought water to the thirsty and bandaged the wounded. Anas tells us that on the Day of *Uhud*, "I saw ᶜA'ishah, the daughter of Abu Bakr, and Umm Sulaim both lifting their dresses up so that I was able to see the ornaments of their legs. They were carrying waterskins on their arms to pour water into the mouths of thirsty people. Then they would go back and refill them and return to pour water into the mouths of the thirsty again."

Umm Sulaim gave her son, Anas ibn Malik to the Prophet, may Allah bless him and grant him peace, so that Anas could serve him. Anas continued to serve the Prophet for ten years and is known as the Servant of the Prophet.

Now, the Muslims experienced days of extreme poverty and hunger in Madinah. They triumphed over these

Umm Sulaim bint Milhan

hard times through patience and the help they gave each other. The Prophet, may Allah bless him and grant him peace, was like a merciful father. He went hungry with his companions and he would not eat or drink alone.

One day, Anas ibn Malik, went to the Prophet and found him sitting with his companions with his stomach bandaged. So Anas asked them, "Why has the Messenger of Allah bandaged his stomach?" They said, "From hunger." So Anas went to Abu Talha and said, "I saw the Messenger of Allah with his stomach wrapped in a bandage out of hunger." Abu Talha felt that things had become serious and told Anas to accompany him to the house so that they could see what was available for the Prophet and his companions.

They went home and Abu Talha asked Umm Sulaim, "What do you have to eat so that we can invite the Prophet and his companions. She looked to see what they had and said, "I have a few loaves of flat bread and some dates. If the Prophet himself, may Allah bless him and grant him peace, comes alone they will fill him. However, if the others come with, that will not be enough for them."

Sorrow appeared on the face of Abu Talha, and he said, "Some loaves of flat bread and dates. What are we going to do? The Messenger of Allah has bandaged his stomach out of hunger and his companions are with him. They have not found enough to satisfy their hunger."

Umm Sulaim was quiet for a moment as she thought, then she said, "We will send Anas to the Prophet to invite him and to inform him of what we have and he can decide what is the best thing to do."

Abu Talha agreed with her. So Anas went and after a time he returned with the Prophet and the people. Abu

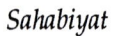

Talha was embarrassed. He turned to Umm Sulaim and said, "The Prophet, may Allah bless him and grant him peace, has come with people and we don't have the wherewithal to feed them."

She answered confidently, "O Abu Talha, Allah and His Prophet know best. Surely, Allah will not shame you in front of your guests, for you are spending from your wealth and yourself in the path of Allah, seeking only His good pleasure."

On that note, Abu Talha left, contentment and relief in his heart, to greet the Prophet and his other guests. The Prophet and Abu Talha soon came back to Umm Sulaim and the Prophet, may Allah bless him and grant him peace, said, "Bring me what you have, O Umm Sulaim." She gave him what food she had and the Prophet, may Allah bless him and grant him peace, prayed to Allah to bless it. Then they gave permission to the people to enter group by group until they had all eaten. Next, the Prophet, may Allah bless him and grant him peace, and his household ate. Yet, after all had eaten, Umm Sulaim and Abu Talha still had food to give to their neighbours.

Abu Talha and Umm Sulaim had a son. Anas tells us that one day this son died. Umm Sulaim said to the members of her family, "Do not tell Abu Talha about his son until I tell him." Abu Talha came home. She gave him his supper, which he took and ate and he drank some water. She dressed and perfumed herself, which she had not done before. Abu Talha made love to her, then she said, "Abu Talha, if some people borrow something from another family and then they ask for its return, would they resist its return?" He said, "No." She said, "I'm telling you about the death of your son." He was annoyed

Umm Sulaim bint Milhan

and said, "You did not inform me until I had made love to you, and then you give me the news about my son." He went to the Messenger of Allah and told him what had happened. The Messenger of Allah, may Allah bless him and grant him peace, said, "May Allah bless both of you in the night spent by you."

Umm Sulaim became pregnant with ᶜAbdullah. Even so, she was present on the Day of *Hunain*. She was very brave and carried a dagger about her waist even though she was pregnant. Abu Talha said to the Prophet, "O Messenger of Allah, Umm Sulaim has a dagger." Umm Sulaim, "O Prophet, I brought this dagger so that if any idolator comes near me, I'll stab him in his stomach. I'll kill those who flee from you as you kill those who are fighting you, and that is what they deserve." The Prophet, may Allah bless him and grant him peace, said, "O Umm Sulaim, surely Allah suffices."

Abu Talha and Umm Sulaim were later accompanying the Messenger of Allah on a journey. When the party came near Madinah, Umm Sulaim felt labour pains. Abu Talha remained with her and the Messenger of Allah, may Allah bless him and grant him peace, carried on with the rest of the group. Abu Talha said, "O Lord, You know that I love to go along with the Messenger of Allah when he goes out and enter along with him when he enters, and I have been detained as You see." In response to this Umm Sulaim said, "Abu Talha, I do not feel (as much pain) as I was feeling before. We can go on." So they carried on, and she felt contractions as they reached Madinah and the child was born.

Anas said, "My mother said to me, 'Anas, none should suckle him until you go to the Messenger of Allah, may

Allah bless him and grant him peace, tomorrow morning.' And when it was morning I carried the baby and went with him to the Messenger of Allah. He said, may Allah bless him and grant him peace, 'This is perhaps the one Umm Sulaim has given birth to.' I said, 'Yes.' I brought the child to him and placed him in his lap and the Messenger of Allah, may Allah bless him and grant him peace, asked that ᶜ*Ajwa* dates of Madinah be brought and he softened them in his mouth. When these had become palatable, he placed them in the mouth of the baby. The baby began to taste them. So the Messenger of Allah, may Allah bless him and grant him peace, said, 'See what love the Ansar have for dates.' Then he wiped his face and named him ᶜAbdullah."

Umm Sulaim was an example of courage, faith, contentment, and wisdom in all spheres, whether on the battlefield of war or in everyday life. The Messenger of Allah, may Allah bless him and grant him peace, said about her, "I entered Paradise and heard the noise of steps. I asked, 'Who is it?' They said, 'She is Ghumaisa, the daughter of Milhan, the mother of Anas ibn Malik.'"